Appaloosa "The Leopard of the Americas"

Horse Books For Kids

Nature Books for Kids

By

K. Bennett

JD-Biz Publishing

Read More Amazing Animal Books

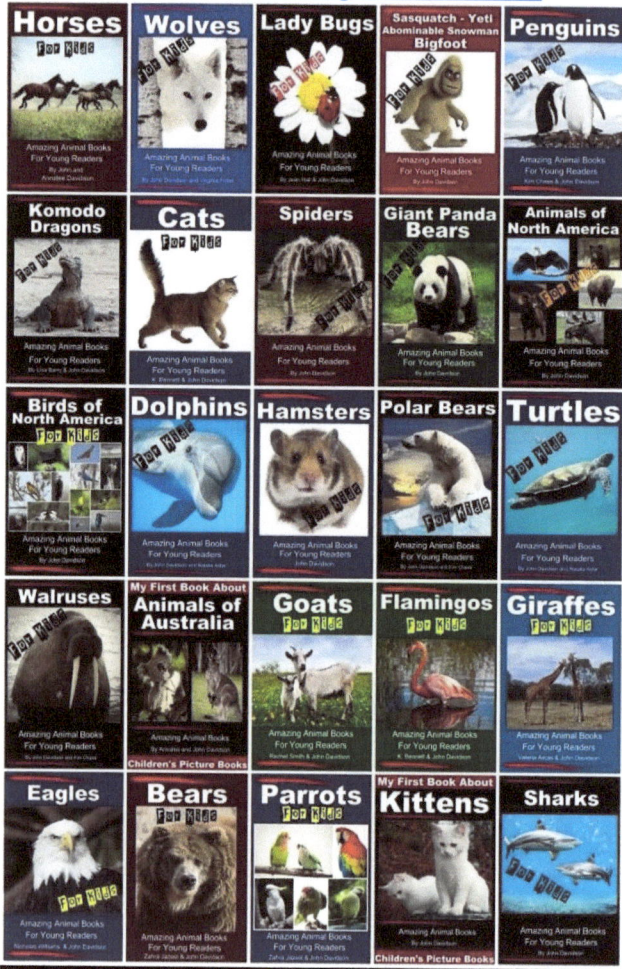

Purchase at Amazon.com

Table of Contents

Introduction

Chapter 1 Great Horses

Chapter 2 Amazing Creatures

Chapter 3 Horse Fun Facts!

Conclusion Nature's Amazing Wonders

Author Bio

Appaloosa

Introduction

***

Appaloosa: Appaloosas are very special horses that come from the American Northwest in the East part of Washington, Oregon and the West part of Idaho. They are strong, beautiful, fast and sure footed. This means they don't trip over their feet very much!

Many years ago, the Nez Perce Indians took care of these beautiful animals. But where did they get them? We learn from history that they got them from the Shoshone tribe around the year 1730.

This trade was great for the Nez Perce Indians and great for the horses too. Why? Because these noble horses changed the lives of the tribe forever! But how did Appaloosa's do that?

At first, the Nez Perce Indians lived a quiet life and they loved to fish in the calm waters, cultivate plants from the ground, gather berries and take care of their families. But when the horses came into their lives, the Nez Perce Indians became strong hunters. They were very good on horses and soon became known as excellent riders.

Appaloosas were a large part of the Nez Perce Indians life, and they took great care of them. When they bred the horses, which simply means have more horse babies, these horses were strong, fast and very smart! Do you know why? Because the Nez Perce took away the weaker horses and left only the strong behind! By the 19th century, Nez Perce Indians were known as great horse breeders.

On February 15, 1806, a man by the name of Meriwether Lewis wrote something nice about the horses of the Nez Perce Indians. He said: *"Their horses appear to be of an excellent race; they are lofty, elegantly formed, active and durable...some of these horses are pided with large spots of white irregularly scattered and intermixed with black, brown, bey or some other dark color."*

It seems Mr. Lewis really loved Appaloosas and he liked the color of their coat! But can you tell what color it is? Look at the horse closely. What colors do you see?

What makes Appaloosas so special?

Appaloosa

The coat color of the Appaloosa is very pretty and different. Underneath you will find a base color and on top something amazing happens. They are beautiful spot patterns all over the horse! Some of the horses may only have these spots on a small part of their body, but others are covered from head to toe!

Where do Appaloosas get their beautiful coat?

This variation has to do with genetics. Do you know what this means? **Sciencekidsathome.com** says this: *"Inside every cell of each living thing (plant or animal) are sets of instructions called genes. The genes provide the instructions on ... the plant or animal, what it looks like, how it is to survive, and how it will interact with its surrounding environment."*

And this is what genetics is. So, in the case of Appaloosas, genetics give them a beautiful coat with lots of spots!

Appaloosas today

Appaloosas are amazing horses and today, it is one of the most popular horses in the United States. Although it is known as a stock horse, it is good at many other things too like: Riding disciplines (We will talk about that later), acting in movies (Yes, they can act too!) and working as a mascot with the Florida State University. It is also the official state horse of Idaho since 1975.

With their unique coat colors, beautiful personality and rich ancestry, Appaloosas are wonderful horses to learn about. Please take a moment to read a little more about this noble animal and don't forget to share what you learn with others!

Hello there!

WOULD YOU LIKE TO DRAW A SIMPLE HORSE? LEARN HERE!

Wikihow.com has a simple, but neat tutorial on drawing horses. Here are the steps to get started:

1- **First,** ask your parent's or a guardian's permission to go online.

2- In your browser (Chrome, Internet explorer, Firefox, Torch) type: www.Wikihow.com

3- In the search box at the top of the page type: *Draw a simple horse.* Once the search is complete, you should see a title that reads: "**How to draw a simple horse: 11 steps with pictures**."

4 – Click on the link and follow the steps.

5- Have fun!

Appaloosa

Chapter 1

Hi, just out for a walk!

History: To understand where this beautiful horse came from, we have to go back in history to prehistoric days. Why so far back? Well, did you know…they found paintings on cave walls that looked like horses with spots? Yes! They did.

The ***Appaloosamuseum.org*** talks about cave paintings from the year 18,000 BC (This means Before Christ) in France. There are some beautiful paintings on the walls that look like horses with lots of spots.

Are these paintings ancestors of the Appaloosas horses?

Science says no. They said these drawings are dreams that people had of horses with spots. That may be true, but the paintings are there and the horses have spots! So, what do you think? Did these ancient people dream about the horses, or did they really "see" spotted horses? Make a choice and come to your own conclusions!

Beautiful coat

China

In the year 100 BC, the emperor Wu Ti sent his officials to find the "Heavenly or Celestial horses." Who were these beautiful horses? We don't really know but guess what? They had spotted coats!

Greece

Ancient Greece also had paintings of these magnificent horses. A beautiful vase was found near a tomb with decorative paintings of warriors and horses with spots!

England

Around the 12th century, English art had beautiful horses with spotted coats! Usually the riders were noble or high ranking people and saints.

Name change

What about the name? Where did it come from? Many years ago this pretty horse was called: "Palouse horse." We do not know where this name came from, but many people believe the settlers named them after a river called "Palouse river," or after the tribe called "Palouse tribe."

Then later, some of the settlers started to call them "A Palouse horse," which changed to "Appalousey." However, in the year 1938 the official name of Appaloosa was given to the horse and we still use the same name today!

What makes this horse different?

Appaloosas have beautiful and exotic coats with amazing names. The **Appaloosa horse club** describes some of the color varieties like this:

-Leopard

-Snowflake

-Marble

-Frost

-Blanket

Which name do you like best? And how is each color different than the rest?

My coat is cute!

Leopard: These horses have a beautiful white body with large, dark spots from head to toe!

Snowflake: They have a darker body with lighter spots or flecks.

Marble: They have smaller spots or flecks over a light coat.

Frost: They have small light flecks covering a darker coat.

Blanket: Their spots are on the hips or loins area. They may also have darker spots on a white blanket. There is one last coat color you might find surprising. It's "solid." This means the Appaloosa doesn't have a coat pattern at all, just a solid color! However, there can also be variations of "solid" colors!

(Source: *Ultimatehorsesite.com*)

So, which color variation do you like? Pick one and tell your parents, classmates or guardian about it… and why you like it!

FUN FACTS FOR KIDS:

Measuring horses: What is **HANDS**?

This is a neat way to measure horses. The measurement refers to hands, literal hands! The symbol is usually HH (Hands high). So you would say 15hh, 16hh or 17hh. This means 15 hands, 16 hands and 17 hands. You might be wondering why people measure horses in hands?

Well, many years ago people did not have rulers or measuring sticks like we do today. So they used whatever they had…and they had hands. So horses are measured like this. You can do it too! How?

Think about it like this: One hand is 4 inches.

So if a horse is 15 hands multiply this by 4. (15 x 4) and you will get 60 inches. And if a horse is 16 hands multiply this number by 4. (16 x 4) and you will get 64 inches.

Now that you know how to do it, you can measure other horses for yourself. Have fun!

This grass is yummier!

Strengths: Appaloosas are great horses with a heart of gold. They are used in many different types of sports. Some of the competitions include: Roping, Reining, Cutting and O-Mok-See. Do you remember what **O-Mok-See** means? In our "*Colonial Spanish for Kids*" book, we wrote about this skill, but I will repeat it again for you!

O-Mok-See means "games on horseback." So a horse and rider play games together! This show is for many people to enjoy and the horse and rider get points for good horsemanship.

It is not only for adults. Kids get to participate too! Would you like to try? How much you learn and how fast you go is up to you. One of the "games on horseback" includes **barrel racing**. Do you know what this type of sport is?

Barrel racing: This type of show has a pattern. A clover leaf pattern. Think about this scene…

The arena is clear…everything nice and clean. 3 barrels are placed in 3 different places. All of a sudden you hear the go and a rider comes at full speed! Vaaaa-rroooommmmm!!! They go as fast as they can and get as close as they can to the barrels… without tipping them over! If you tip the barrel you lose points, but if you leave them standing, you gain points.

How long should this take? You have 60 seconds for the event and it depends on the arena, space and more…but the winning speed should be around 13 to 14 seconds!

How long is that? Count one Mississippi, two Mississippi, three Mississippi, four Mississippi…and when you get to 14 stop. There! That's how long it would take. Can you ride fast like that?

The winner is the fastest rider so you have to beat the clock to get the prize.

Don't forget you don't just ride in a straight line…remember the clover? Yes! It's a pattern, so you have to respect it and ride in three different directions. Think of a triangle and you will get the idea.

On your mark…Get set….Go!

Now that we know about Barrel racing, what else do we have? In the English disciplines, Appaloosas are great at: Show jumping, eventing and even fox hunting. Do you remember what eventing is? In our "*Akhal Teke for Kids*" book, we wrote about this skill, but let me refresh your memory!

Eventing: Another name for this sport is "Horse trials." Riders and horses compete in different events. It includes 3 types of events in one. Cross country, dressage and show jumping. Another word for this is Triathlon. You probably know that triathlon means 3! So this is 3 competitions at one time.

The competition can last for one, two or three days depending on the rules. But to be chosen, both horse and rider need to pass a test at the beginning! Usually, both horse and rider look their best to impress the judges.

Weaknesses: With such an amazing horse, do you think they have

weaknesses? Sadly, yes! We all get to a point where we can't do some activity or thing we would like to do, right? The same happens to Appaloosas. They have a big problem with their eyes and many of them go blind. This is called: *Equine Recurrent Uveitis*. If this sounds strange think about this term: **Moon blindness.**

Sadly, it affects the Appaloosas eyes. They also get sick from something else called: CSNB, which is "congenital stationary night blindness." This problem only affects them at night. During the day, they can see just fine but at night, it's a different story!

Yum! Yum! Mommy, can I try it too?

Characteristics: Appaloosas have lots of different body types. Some are big and some are small. Why are they so different? Because they were mixed with different types of horses!

Height: Approximately 14 to 16 hands.

Weight: 950-1250 pounds. Some may weigh a little more or less, but this is the usual weight.

Coats: Appaloosas have beautiful coat colors, which we talked about before. But there is more! The Appaloosa horse club includes other colors like: Bay, roan, grulla, dun, cremello and gray! Do you remember what ***Roan*** means?

Appaloosa

Roan: Is more than one color. It is a pattern of colors with a mixture of white. The horse will have lots of white hairs mixed with their other hairs. Generally, this applies to the head, lower legs, mane and tail. They are more solid or will have fewer white hairs. Sometimes, this color variation is called Silvery. Isn't that beautiful?

Chapter 2

The view is nice up here!

Have you learned anything new about Appaloosas? Wonderful! But there is still a little bit more we can learn about them. How about training? We will detail the steps for training all horses and then give you additional tips on training Appaloosas! Ready?

Training: *Wikihow* recommends the following steps to train horses:

1-***First of all, don't scare the horse***. That means you should not run up or sneak up on them suddenly. This is not a hard to understand. For example, do you like it when people run or sneak up on you suddenly?

It may scare you when someone does that, right? Then a horse will feel the same way.

2-*Be gentle and talk gently to your horse*. There is no need to yell, shout or talk in a harsh tone to your horse. Again, this idea is not hard to understand. Do you like it when people talk to you gently? Or do you want them to shout and yell at you? Isn't it nicer to treat others kindly and don't you appreciate it when others do the same for you? Your horse will appreciate your kind manner too!

3-*Most horses love to be touched*. Show them your feelings through your hands. Stroke them on the head, massage their neck, hug them, brush them and communicate your affection through gentle fingers. Imagine how happy your horse will be!

4-*Try to spend as much time as you can with your horse*. In any friendship, regular visits are the key! No matter what you have to do, stop by and visit your horse just to remind them that you're there. They will be so happy to see you and the more you spend time with them, the stronger your bond will grow.

5- *A nice reward*. A tasty treat, rub or pat down, yummy food, grooming of whatever other treat you might have in mind, will be a great idea! Do this at the end of the day to let your horse know how much you enjoyed spending time with them.

Wild and Free!

Appaloosa training skills: It is good to understand that Appaloosas, unlike other horse breeds, can be a bit hard to handle. Why? Well, just like us, they have good days and bad days! And on the bad days, they may be unhappy and not willing to work. Some of them may be stubborn too!

April Reeves from ***Aprilreeveshorsetraining.wordpress.com*** says it best when she writes: "***The horse you lead is the horse you ride.***" So, the right training goes a long way to having a nice, responsible horse!

She lists the most important ingredients to train your Appaloosa.

Appaloosa

-Consistency

-Timing

-Repetition

-Patience and

-Calm!

She also says: "Stay persistent and consistent." With these tips in mind, you will have a happy, confident and loving horse!

CURIOUS FACT FOR KIDS:

Horses, like us, have different titles for different stages of life. For example when a horse is born until 6 months of age it is called a *foal*.

Then up to the age of 2 years it is called a *yearling*. If the horse is a male horse it is called a *colt* under the age of 4. When it is older than 4 years it is called a *stallion*. Do you remember what a Stallion is?

<u>Meaning of Terms:</u>

A **stallion** is a: Male horse that can have kids.

A **gelding** is a: Male horse that cannot have kids. (Geldings are usually patient, calm, quiet and well behaved.)

A young female horse or pony is called **filly** and after the age of 4, she is called a **mare**. (Source: **Lessonpaths.com**)

So much fun to run!

Chapter 3

Training a horse is a great, but knowing what horses are like is also great. This will help you to understand what is going on behind their bright, curious eyes! Think about this:

-A horse can express its emotions in many different ways. It can use its face, eyes and ears to tell you how it feels!

-Horses are great at keeping watch. It is rare to see a herd with everyone snoozing at one time. There is usually one horse standing as a lookout, and his job is to warn the others if danger comes near!

- Avoid standing behind a horse. They have great vision, but there are a couple of blind spots. Can you guess what the back part of the horse is? Yes! It's a blind spot. If the horse gets angry or scared, guess what he might do if you stand directly behind him?

-Horses are great at listening! They can turn their ears in different ways to improve their hearing. If you whisper and say something bad about your horse, they just might hear you!

- Horses can help people get better when they have mental or health problems. This is called: *Equine Assisted Therapy*.

-Horses are the best sleepers on the planet. They can sleep lying down and standing up! Can you do that?

- Horses are herbivores. Do you know that this means? It means they eat plants or are plant eaters, if you like this term better.

-Horses have feelings and emotions too! Treat them kindly with lots of patience and love. You may be surprised at the results!

(Source: *Onekind.org*)

INTERESTING FACT FOR KIDS:

Appaloosas have a unique coat color called a "***Leopard complex***." But this color spreads to other parts of their body like the hooves. Did you know they are stripped? Even the eyes are different than other horses.

Because of their "Leopard Complex," Appaloosa's have lots of different body types. But this is also because of different types of crossbreeding. Do you remember what crossbreeding means?

The dictionary at Kids.Net.Au defines this word like this: "*(genetics) the act of mixing different species or varieties of animals or plants and thus to produce hybrids.*"

Appaloosa

So they mixed the horses together to make a new horse! These horses included Spanish, Arabian and American Quarter horses. Even Thoroughbreds were added to the mix to make a stronger, race horse.

The "***Leopard Complex***" is an interesting subject to study about. Would you like to try to learn more about it? Then ask your parent or a guardian's permission and do some research on the subject!

Will you be my friend?

Appaloosa

Conclusion:

In conclusion: Horses are beautiful creatures, and Appaloosas are no different! This strong, loyal and intelligent horse is a wonderful example of how amazing Earth's creatures can be.

This is a great time to learn a bit more about these noble animals. You may be amazed at what you can discover. If you don't know where to look, ask your teacher, a parent or guardian to help you. They may have some great ideas too!

If you don't know exactly what to research about this noble breed, then think about this: Why don't you choose something you really like (It can be the tail, mane, ears, body, size, personality, history, etc) and learn a bit more about that particular subject?

In the case of Appaloosas, you could research how they are so important to American culture. For example: Did you know Appaloosas were a part of TV shows like "Cojo Rojo?" What about the Marlon Brando movie "The Appaloosa?" But wait, there's more!

John Wayne acted in the 1966 movie called "El Dorado" and he rode a beautiful horse named "Zip Cochise." Matt Damon acted in "True Grit" and rode a horse named "Cowboy." I am sure there are other shows and movies out there that feature Appaloosas! Perhaps you know some of them yourself.

Another option is this: If you are in school and you participate in show and tell, use that as your subject. Many of your classmates may not even know what an Appaloosa is really like, so it would be nice to share what you find with others!

I hope this book has taught you just a little on how wonderful nature is, and how each creature can impact our life in amazing ways.

 And remember: *"Educating the mind without educating the heart is no education at all."* - *Aristotle*

Author Bio

K. Bennett loves to write for both children and adults. Many different subjects are interesting to develop, but writing for children is special to her heart.

Her favorite pastimes include reading, traveling and discovering new things. Each of these activities helps to fuel her imagination and acts like a blank canvas waiting for more stories.

She is intrigued with fantasy elements like hidden worlds and faraway lands. Basically anything that gets her imagination soaring to new heights!

Her writing credits include children books online, short stories for online magazines, and two novellas listed at Amazon.com

Our books are available at

1. Amazon.com

2. Barnes and Noble

3. Itunes

4. Kobo

5. Smashwords

6. Google Play Books

Publisher

JD-Biz Corp

P O Box 374

Mendon, Utah 84325

http://www.jd-biz.com/

Appaloosa

Appaloosa

Appaloosa

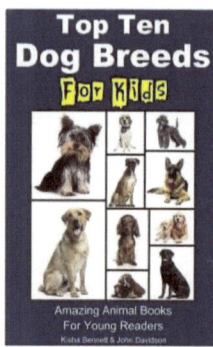

Top Ten Dog Breeds For Kids

Amazing Animal Books For Young Readers

Krisha Bennett & John Davidson

German Shepherds

Dog Books for Kids

K. Bennett

Bulldogs

Dog Books for Kids

K. Bennett

Dachshund

Dog Books for Kids

K. Bennett

Poodles

Dog Books for Kids

K. Bennett

Labrador Retrievers

Dog Books for Kids

K. Bennett

Rottweilers

Dog Books for Kids

K. Bennett

Boxers

Dog Books for Kids

K. Bennett

Golden Retrievers

Dog Books for Kids

K. Bennett

Puppies

Dog Books For Kids

Amazing Animal Books

By John Davidson

Beagles

Dog Books for Kids

K. Bennett

Yorkshire Terriers

Dog Books for Kids

K. Bennett

Dogs Top Ten Dog Breeds For Kids

Amazing Animal Books For Young Readers

Zahra Jazeel & John Davidson

Cats For Kids

Amazing Animal Books For Young Readers

K. Bennett & John Davidson

Foxes For Kids

Amazing Animal Books For Young Readers

Zahra Jazeel & John Davidson

Wolves For Kids

Amazing Animal Books For Young Readers

By John Davidson and Virginia Fidler

Appaloosa

Monkeys
Amazing Animal Books
For Young Readers
By John and
Annalee Davidson

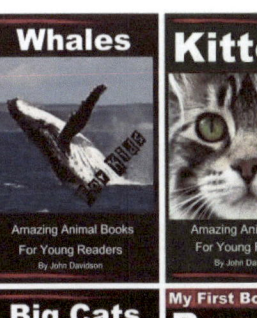

Whales
Amazing Animal Books
For Young Readers
By John Davidson

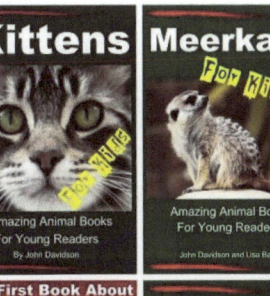

Kittens
Amazing Animal Books
For Young Readers
By John Davidson

Meerkats
Amazing Animal Books
For Young Readers
John Davidson and Lisa Barry

Elephants
Amazing Animal Books
For Young Readers
Kim Chase & John Davidson

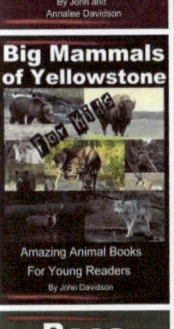

Big Mammals of Yellowstone
Amazing Animal Books
For Young Readers
By John Davidson

Big Cats
Amazing Animal Books
For Young Readers
By John Davidson

My First Book About Pandas
Amazing Animal Books
By Annalee and John Davidson
BEST
Children's Picture Books

Chinchillas
Amazing Animal Books
For Young Readers
John Davidson and Jaimie Rhynsburger

Beavers
Amazing Animal Books
For Young Readers
By J Davidson

Bees
Amazing Animal Books
For Young Readers
By J Davidson and Jennifer Lejeune

Animals of Australia
Amazing Animal Books
For Young Readers
By John Davidson
and Shawn Vincent Wilson

Frogs
Amazing Animal Books
For Young Readers
By John Davidson

My First Book About Frogs
Amazing Animal Books
By John Davidson
Children's Picture Books

Tigers
Amazing Animal Books
For Young Readers
Kim Chase & John Davidson

Scorpions
Amazing Animal Books
For Young Readers
John Davidson

Snakes
Amazing Animal Books
For Young Readers
By John Davidson and Nadine Thieie

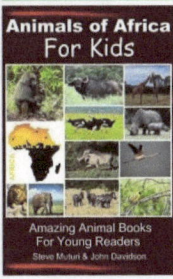

Animals of Africa
For Kids
Amazing Animal Books
For Young Readers
Steve Muturi & John Davidson

Dinosaurs
Amazing Animal Books
For Young Readers
By John Davidson

Sharks
Amazing Animal Books
For Young Readers
By John Davidson

Spiders
Amazing Animal Books
For Young Readers
By John Davidson

Giant Panda Bears
Amazing Animal Books
For Young Readers
By John Davidson

Giraffes
For Kids
Amazing Animal Books
For Young Readers
Valeria Arcas & John Davidson

Eagles
Amazing Animal Books
For Young Readers
Nicholas Williams & John Davidson

Bears
For Kids
Amazing Animal Books
For Young Readers
Zahra Jazeel & John Davidson

Appaloosa

Horses For Kids
Amazing Animal Books For Young Readers
By John and Annalee Davidson

Wolves For Kids
Amazing Animal Books For Young Readers
By John Davidson and Virginia Fidler

Lady Bugs For Kids
Amazing Animal Books For Young Readers
By Jean Hall & John Davidson

Sasquatch - Yeti Abominable Snowman Bigfoot For Kids
Amazing Animal Books For Young Readers
By John Davidson

Penguins For Kids
Amazing Animal Books For Young Readers
Kim Chase & John Davidson

Komodo Dragons For Kids
Amazing Animal Books For Young Readers
By Lisa Barry & John Davidson

Cats For Kids
Amazing Animal Books For Young Readers
K. Bennett & John Davidson

Spiders For Kids
Amazing Animal Books For Young Readers
By John Davidson

Giant Panda Bears For Kids
Amazing Animal Books For Young Readers
By John Davidson

Animals of North America For Kids
Amazing Animal Books For Young Readers
By John Davidson

Birds of North America For Kids
Amazing Animal Books For Young Readers
By John Davidson

Dolphins For Kids
Amazing Animal Books For Young Readers
By John Davidson and Natasa Asfar

Hamsters For Kids
Amazing Animal Books For Young Readers
John Davidson

Polar Bears For Kids
Amazing Animal Books For Young Readers
By John Davidson and Kim Chase

Turtles For Kids
Amazing Animal Books For Young Readers
By John Davidson and Natasa Asfar

Walruses For Kids
Amazing Animal Books For Young Readers
By John Davidson and Kim Chase

My First Book About Animals of Australia For Kids
Amazing Animal Books
By Annalee and John Davidson
Children's Picture Books

Goats For Kids
Amazing Animal Books For Young Readers
Rachel Smith & John Davidson

Flamingos For Kids
Amazing Animal Books For Young Readers
K. Bennett & John Davidson

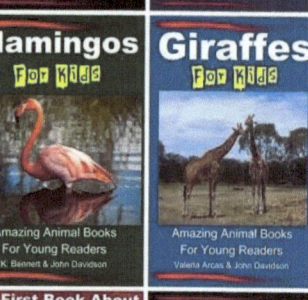
Giraffes For Kids
Amazing Animal Books For Young Readers
Valeria Arcas & John Davidson

Eagles For Kids
Amazing Animal Books For Young Readers
Nicholas Williams & John Davidson

Bears For Kids
Amazing Animal Books For Young Readers

Parrots For Kids
Amazing Animal Books For Young Readers
Zahra Jazeel & John Davidson

My First Book About Kittens For Kids
Amazing Animal Books
By John Davidson
Children's Picture Books

Sharks For Kids
Amazing Animal Books For Young Readers
By John Davidson

Appaloosa

www.ingramcontent.com/pod-product-compliance
Lightning Source LLC
Chambersburg PA
CBHW050850290526
45792CB00002B/592